# Wild Flowers of the Midwest

Illinois
Indiana
Iowa
Kansas
Michigan
Minnesota
Missouri
Nebraska
North Dakota
Ohio
South Dakota
Wisconsin

CO-BPA-070

Tundra Books                    Katherine Mackenzie

A book about wild flowers should be as beautiful as the flowers themselves, and Katherine Mackenzie's lovely watercolors, executed with so much care and love, make **Wild Flowers of the Midwest** far more than the usual field guide.

The 100 wild flowers reproduced in 90 full color plates will, of course, be referred to avidly by those who can barely tell their buttercups from their "butter-and-eggs," but even the longtime naturalist will find much to delight in. All of the paintings were made from living flowers and they capture the distinctive features of each as well as the individual vitality and charm, usually ignored in technical books.

For newcomers to the wonderful world of wild flowers, and especially for children, the descriptive texts give intriguing bits of information, history, superstitions, ancient food uses that show how aware our Indian forerunners were of wild flowers — all intended to make the search the delight it should be.

Copyright ©1973, Katherine Mackenzie
New material ©1976,
Katherine Mackenzie

ISBN 0-912766-33-6
ISBN (12 pre-pack) 0-912766-40-9
Library of Congress Card No. 75-44840

Published by Tundra Books of Northern New York, Plattsburgh, N.Y. 12901
Printed in the United States.

## A Note from the Author

I am neither a botanist nor an artist. All of the flowers in this book were painted for my own private pleasure. I have explored for wild flowers since childhood but it was only eight years ago that I looked for a way of preserving them. I bought a press to flatten and dry them, but the first afternoon I tried to use it, I hated the result. The flowers looked so dead. Disappointed, I went out into my garden and stood looking at a Forget-me-not, alive and growing. I decided to try to draw and paint it. That was the beginning. Since then my search has taken me as far north as the Arctic Circle, and I am now at work on a collection of flowers of the Southern States.

I wish I could introduce everyone, and especially every child, to the unique joy of searching for wild flowers, and of finding the rarer ones, particularly the wild orchids. It is like coming across an endangered species of exotic bird, still wild and free. One feels somehow privileged.

## Acknowledgments

Several botanists have assisted me in identifying the flowers in this book. Unfortunately, in a few cases - such as the goldenrod, the blue violet and the wild cherry - where many species exist with very slight variations between them, absolute identification was not possible, and I have used the family name only.

I particularly want to thank Dr. Edward G. Voss, curator and professor at the University of Michigan Herbarium in Ann Arbor for his kindness in making many helpful criticisms and suggestions concerning both text and identification. The final choice of flowers and the final decision about names, English and Latin, are, however, my own. I have used as reference mainly Gray's **Manual of Botany** but I also found helpful the Peterson and McKenny's **Guides.**

# 1 Blue Violet
Viola

This popular violet blooms in early spring. You can find recipes for sugaring violets so that you can preserve them and even eat them, but I prefer to look at them.

## Smooth Yellow Violet
Viola pensylvanica

This little violet grows from six to twelve inches high in the woods and fields in spring and early summer. It is not as common as the blue.

The violet is the state flower of Illinois, Rhode Island and New Jersey.

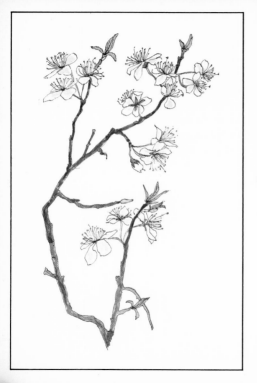

## 2 Wild Cherry
Prunus

This lovely wild cherry is a small tree. It likes a sunny spot, but isn't fussy about the soil. The sight of cherry trees in spring has inspired much poetry, and certainly the large blossoms look lovely amid the fresh greens of the newly budding trees around it. The red berries that come out at the end of summer are very sour but edible. They make excellent preserves.

### 3 Sharp-lobed Hepatica
Hepatica acutiloba

Another herald of spring in northern
climates is the dainty hepatica growing up
to just about six inches through the old
wet leaves in heavily wooded areas. It is
a member of the buttercup family, but
its flowers come in white, pink, lavender
or blue. Some have a sweet smell, but
you have to bend close to find out which.

## 4 Wild Ginger
Asarum canadense

At first glance, the heart-shaped leaves are all that will be seen when you come upon a stand of Wild Ginger in May or June, but if you look under the leaves you will find the little red-brown flower. Sometimes you even have to scrape away the dried leaves. The plant grows in rich woods and the fascinating little flower is at ground level. An oil found in the root is used in making perfume.

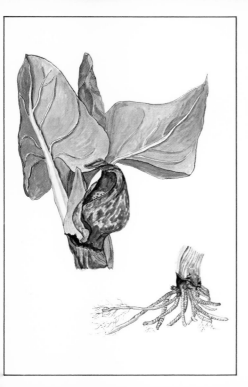

## 5 Skunk Cabbage
Symplocarpus foetidus

The skunk cabbage — called in French "the devil's tobacco" — is given its bad names because of the odor the leaves give off when crushed. It is the first plant to appear in spring while the snow is still on the ground because it gets a headstart in autumn when the spathe is formed. The hood surrounding the flower is a shell-like sheath of purple-brown streaked with yellow. It grows in very wet sandy places, and when the flowers die down late in the spring, bright green fruits appear. It is a plant that can live as long as seventy-five years.

## 6 Dutchman's-breeches
Dicentra cucullaria

Another charming inhabitant of the rich
woods in early spring is Dutchman's-
breeches, so-called because each of the
delicate waxy yellow-topped flowers looks
like a tiny pair of blown-up pantaloons
attached at the waist to the stem. It
grows to a height of twelve inches and
has a fragrant smell and fern-like leaves.

## 7 Dogtooth Violet or Trout-lily
Erythronium americanum

This lovely little yellow lily, another first flower of spring, can be found carpeting the ground under trees in rich woods. The bulbs multiply underground, breaking up through dark wet mold in masses of flowers. Cattle love the leaves and the Indians used to make a tea of them which relieved stomach pains. It grows only four to ten inches high.

## Large-flowered Bellwort
Uvularia grandiflora

The bellwort is sometimes called the "wood daffodil," because of its rich yellow, bell-shaped flowers, a striking sight in the spring woods. A native North American plant, it was described as early as 1635 in *Canadensium Plantarum Historia.* The Indians boiled the root to cure backache.

## 8 Trailing Arbutus
Epigaea repens

Sometimes called Mayflower, the Trailing Arbutus has pale pink, sweet-smelling blossoms hidden under the leaves. It must not be picked because this loosens the roots. Look for it in rocky acid woods, especially under pine trees in early spring. Later in the season when the flowers are over, the leaves are easily recognized for their leathery, rusty look. Ants love to eat the fruit. This is a really beautiful plant well worth looking for, and you can find it anywhere in northern climates.

## 9 Painted Trillium
*Trillium undulatum*

This exquisitely lovely white trillium with the crimson heart will immediately attract your attention in the spring woods if you are anywhere near it. And when you find one, you will usually find a few more. But don't pick any, as they are very precious and dying out. They come up with the first green shoots of spring before the trees have enough leaves to block out all sunlight. It's the nicest — and easiest — time to walk in the woods anyway.

## 10 White Trillium
Trillium grandiflorum

It is forbidden by law in some states
to pick trilliums, and this law should
apply everywhere, for the sight of a
wooded mountain side covered with
white trilliums — once the loveliest sign
of spring in northern woods — is passing.
Because they can seem plentiful, white
trilliums give the impression that they
are tough to destroy. But this is not so,
and unless we are careful, these magnifi-
cent twelve-inch plants may become
only a memory. Their roots have been
used by the old herbalists to make
medicine for stomach disorders, rheumatism and earache.

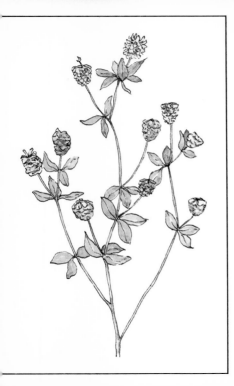

## 11 Hop Clover
Trifolium agrarium

This yellow clover came over from Europe, like most of our clovers but — unlike most of our clovers — it is not liked by cattle. Its bright flowers give a sunny touch to fields and waste places where many other wild flowers refuse to grow. It blooms from June through summer. Toward September most of its flowers have become brownish; as these wither, the florets fold down and look like dried hops — hence its English name. Its Latin name means "of the fields."

## 12 Jewel-weed or Spotted Touch-me-not
Impatiens capensis

Jewel-weed is as beautiful as its name.
When you come upon it in August while
walking near a stream or in a damp area,
you'll think you've found a rare and exotic
plant. Exotic it is, but fortunately not rare.
The flowers stand out, as if suspended in
space; they're orange spotted with brown.
Don't try to pick them as they collapse
immediately. But children have always
enjoyed this plant, for the small seed-
pod pops open when touched.

## 13 Foamflower
Tiarella cordifolia

Another dweller of the damp rich woods,
blooming in May and June, is the Foam-
flower. The starry appearance of the tiny
white flowers makes the plant look as if
it is dancing in the dark woods. This is
a very delicate and pretty plant, growing
six inches to a foot high, and has maple-
like leaves.

## 14 Marsh-marigold
*Caltha palustris*

The golden yellow flowers of the Marsh-marigold light up the streams and ditches where it grows and blooms. The fresh young green leaves can be eaten, but must be well cooked. The roots, when boiled, have been used for curing sores. Although it is difficult to transplant the Marsh-marigold — the roots grow in muddy water and must be carefully dug up and placed in similar conditions — if you succeed, the plant will multiply profusely. It is a member of the buttercup family, but the flowers are much larger than true buttercups.

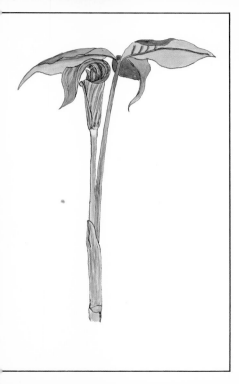

## 15 Jack-in-the-pulpit
Arisaema

Also called Indian Turnip or Bog Onion.
The tube of the spathe (pulpit) is often
deeply corrugated with green and purple
stripes curving all the way to the tip of
the hood. If we call it the "petit prêcheur"
as the French Canadians do, it becomes a
more fitting name for a rare and attractive arum family member. Its sermon
could be a muffled "Don't Pick Me,"
from which we could all take the hint,
for most spring wild flowers are of
some scarcity.

## 16 Pepperroot, Toothwort, Pepperwort
Dentaria diphylla

The taste of the underground stem gave this plant its name. The Indians ground it to make pepper; small boys chew it for its flavor. The plant grows about a foot high in rich deciduous woods. The white flowers bloom in May and June.

### Water avens
Geum rivale

In wet fields, bogs and ditches, from late May until August, the brownish purple flower of the Water Avens is a frequent sight. It grows one or two feet tall, and is actually a member of the rose family. The roots are sometimes boiled to make a sweet tea.

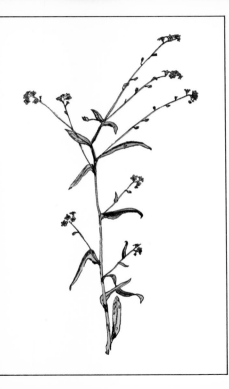

## 17 Forget-me-not
Myosotis laxa

This plant that may grow as little as six inches high, but sometimes reaches two feet, is familiar to everyone who walks by brooks and wet fields in June. It is such an appealing sky-blue flower that I do not find it strange that it should have been the first flower I ever painted, and was then encouraged to go on to the others. While I have avoided quoting the voluminous verse associated with flowers, the one describing how the Forget-me-not got its name is, I think, little known but charming. When God was giving names to the flowers, a little blue-eyed one came meekly forth and said:

"Dear Lord, the name Thou gavest me,
Alas, I have forgot."
Kindly the Father looked Him down
and said, "Forget-me-not."

## 18 Purple Clematis
Clematis verticillaris

An early blooming vine that grows on fences and hedges, in the woods and by the roadside. The lovely purple bell-shaped flower blooms in early June; later the seeds form into a silky ball and make the vine a very pretty sight.

## 19 Indian Cucumber-root
Medeola virginiana

There are two whorls of leaves on this plant, one halfway up the stem and one at the top. Little greenish flowers grow from the top group in May and June, and later dark-purple berries appear. It grows from one to three feet tall in rich woods, especially near cedars. The root does not resemble a cucumber but it is supposed to have a cucumber taste, and may be eaten when marinated in vinegar. It has also been used to make bread. As it is nowhere very abundant, it should never be picked.

## 20 Starflower
Trientalis borealis

It is a pleasure to come upon this delicate flower early in the spring in moist woods, for it is hard to find. But when you do find it, it is likely to be abundant. The seven-petalled star-like flowers grow out of a circle of five to nine pointed leaves at the top of an eight or nine-inch stem. Look for it in cool woods and on high northern mountains.

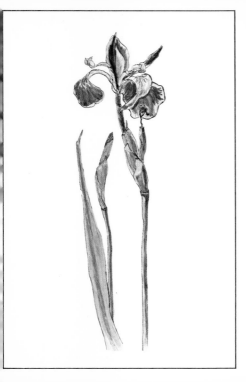

## 21 Larger Blue Flag - Wild Blue Iris
Iris versicolor

This graceful wild iris grows on the edge of lakes, ponds, ditches and wet fields. Its beautiful purply-blue flower — similar to the cultivated iris — makes it visible for some distance. The plant is named for Iris, the attendant to Juno who represented the rainbow.

## 22 Naked Miterwort
Mitella nuda

The Naked Miterwort has exquisitely delicate, deeply fringed petals that identify the plant. The flowers are greenish-yellow.

## One-flowered Wintergreen
Moneses uniflora

This little Wintergreen is like a single jewel growing in the dark woods. The lone waxy white flower (sometimes pink) stands only a few inches high and looks down at its evergreen leaves.

## Starry False Solomon's-seal
Smilacina stellata

Smaller than False Solomon's-seal, the starry flower is larger and grows from the end of the stalk in moist fields, damp woods and on sand dunes. The berries are black.

## 23 Green-headed Coneflower
Rudbeckia laciniata

This very graceful member of the sunflower family can be found in thickets and fields blooming from July to September across the northern United States. Its Latin name comes from Olaf Rudbeck, who was professor of botany at Upsala, Sweden from 1692 until 1740. It is called coneflower because of its cone-shaped center.

## 24 Silvery Cinquefoil
Potentilla argentea

This little five to twelve-inch Cinquefoil (i.e. five-fingers) grows in dry places along roadsides and blooms with a little yellow flower in May and June. Note the five-parted leaves.

## White Sweet Clover
Melilotus alba

It doesn't look like the conventional clover because the flowers taper off, rather than rounding off. It came to us from Europe and was soon naturalized. Its leaves are fragrant, and it can grow as high as six or eight feet, usually in waste, dry and abandoned places like the edges of railway tracks and vacant lots. It is an excellent source of clover honey, and has a long blooming season from May to September.

## 25 Clintonia, Corn-Lily
Clintonia borealis

The Clintonia, or Corn-Lily, or Blue-bead Lily, is not a plant you are likely to miss when walking in coniferous woods. Although it stands only a foot or so high, the shiny green leaves and small greenish bells are striking, particularly if the sun catches them through the trees. The young leaves, when just unrolling, can be eaten raw in salads and have a cucumber-like flavor. They are particularly enjoyed by deer. When the flowers are over, the dark blue berries that take their place can make the Clintonia seem even more beautiful. Hunters used to rub their traps with its roots because the odor these give off is particularly attractive to bears. The plant was named after DeWitt Clinton, a former governor of New York State.

## 26 Canada Anemone
Anemone canadensis

The Canada Anemone is a prolific plant, growing in masses along railway tracks, on beaches and in open, wet woods. The pure white flowers centered with yellow bloom from June to August, and the plant stands about two feet high. It is found quite far north and southwards as far as winter stretches. A tea made from the roots was believed to have soothed lung diseases. The ground-up roots were used by the Indians to stop bleeding.

## 27 Swamp Laurel
*Kalmia polifolia*

Swamp laurel grows, as its name suggests, in bogs and marshy places. It is very similar to sheep laurel except that its flowers are clustered on the ends of the branches, rather than lower down, and are a paler pink.

## 28 Dandelion
Taraxacum officinale

If it wasn't that dandelions like to grow on lawns more than any other place, they might be considered our most valuable wild flower. And if you can lay aside your prejudice, a field of yellow dandelions in the early June sun is quite a dazzling sight. Its uses are many. The flowers are used for dandelion wine. The fresh spring leaves are used in salads, and are now grown for marketing. Our pioneers made a laxative from the root which, today, is used to make a caffein-free coffee. An interesting superstition that children have passed on for generations is that if you pick a dandelion, you will wet the bed that night, hence the French name *pissenlit.*

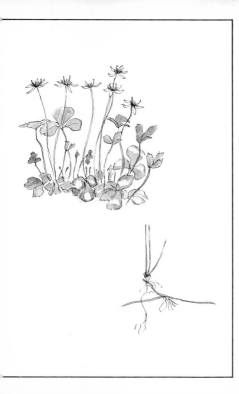

## 29 Goldthread
Coptis groenlandica

This little plant stands only four inches high. Look for the tiny white flowers in deep rich cedar woods in June and July. The French name for the plant is **savoyane,** which, in turn, is an abbreviation of the Micmac word **tisavoyane,** which means "dye for skins."

If you dig down into the moss with your fingers, you will find what looks like a golden wire. This is the underground stem of Goldthread, giving the plant its name. The boiled stem has also been used as a tonic, an antiseptic, and as a cure for stomach-ache.

## 30 Wild Sarsaparilla
Aralia nudicaulis

The wild sarsaparilla blooms in May and June but its greenish-white flowers are sheltered by its leaves and hard to see. The berries that appear later are purple-black. It grows about two feet high in the woods. The roots were made into a popular patent medicine in pioneer days, as well as into a solution that was applied to horses' legs in cases of exhaustion. Indians also used the root as an emergency food.

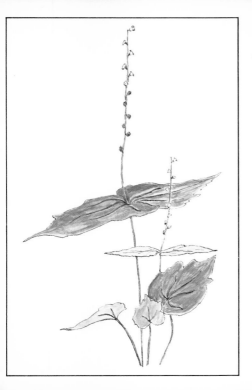

## 31 Two-leaved Miterwort
Mitella diphylla

The Two-leaved Miterwort differs from
the Naked Miterwort (22) in that its stalk
has two stalkless leaves growing just below
the white-fringed flowers, and it is taller by
a foot. Look for it from early spring on in
rich woods. When the blossom period is
over, shiny black seeds are enclosed in a
capsule that resembles a bishop's miter,
hence the name Miterwort.

### 32 Wild Lily-of-the-valley
Maianthemum canadense

A very pretty little three to six-inch plant, flowering in June in the woods. The white berries turn pale red and are food for chipmunks and mice.

### Bunchberry
Cornus canadensis

In June, the greenish-white Bunchberry flowers unfold above its whorl of six leaves, later to be replaced by brilliant red berries much loved by birds.

### Meadow Chickweed
Cerastium arvense

This tiny plant, with white flowers, grows in fields and on rocky land in June. If you count its petals quickly, you will come up with ten, but there are only five, each split almost to its base.

### 33 Red-berried Elder
Sambucus pubens

This shrub has lovely pinkish white blossoms, but they do not smell very good. Look for it in woods and rocky places. The red berry is not edible, by humans that is. Birds love it. The berries appear by mid-summer; this is a much earlier blooming and fruiting species than the common elder.

## 34 Marsh Cinquefoil
*Potentilla palustris*

Most cinquefoils are yellow, but the Marsh Cinquefoil has a red-purple flower that gives the wet fields where it blooms a distinctive color from June to August. It stands one to two feet high in ditches and swamps, and can be recognized by its distinctive leaves which are five to seven-fingered and toothed.

## 35 A Summer Bouquet

Nothing announces the arrival of summer like the **Daisy** (Chrysanthemum leucanthemum). The wild flower of love, it is used for daisy chains and games of "He loves me; he loves me not." And what is so pretty twined around daisies as the lovely purple **Cow Vetch** (Vicia cracca)? Cows love the honey flavor of vetch.

But they hate the taste of fresh **Buttercups** (Ranunculus acris) — although they will eat them dried as fodder. Children say that if you hold a buttercup to the chin, and the skin turns yellow, it means you like butter.

Cows also love **Red Clover** (Trifolium pratense), and a field of it with the bumblebees buzzing around gives both the sound and smell of summer. It is Vermont's state flower.

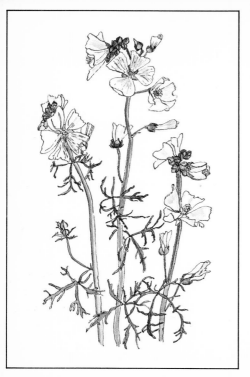

## 36 Musk Mallow
Malva moschata

The Musk Mallow was brought over from Europe as a garden flower, but escaped to the open fields and roadsides to become one of the most decorative of our so-called weeds. It can grow from one to two feet tall.

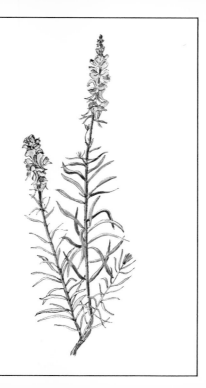

## 37 Butter-and-eggs
Linaria vulgaris

Called "Butter-and-eggs" in English because of the pale yellow and orange snapdragonlike flowers, it grows up to three feet tall by roadsides, in open fields and waste places. Only bees are heavy enough to open the corolla and fertilize the flower, although butterflies keep trying. An ointment made from the root was once used to cure hemorrhoids. Thoreau writes of seeing it one June 19th.

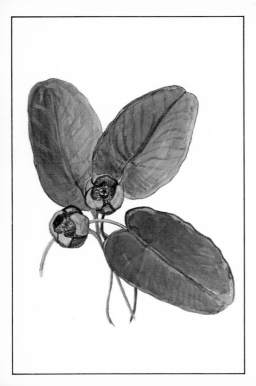

## 38 Bullhead Lily — Red Spatterdock
Nuphar variegatum

A familiar sight in our northern lakes all summer long is the floating yellow water-lily. The thick rootstock, resembling banana stalks, contains large amounts of starch and was boiled and roasted as a vegetable by the Indians. Beaver and moose feed on the roots. It likes inlets of lakes, ponds and protected water.

## 39 False Hellebore — Indian Poke
Veratrum viride

The ribbed leaves of False Hellebore come up early in spring, usually when the snow is still on the ground. Later the plant can grow as high as eight feet with masses of small star-shaped green flowers appearing in late June and July. It favors wet woods, swamps and ditches, and its leaves can cause your skin to sting. All parts of the plant are poisonous.

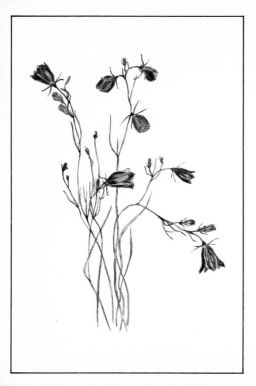

## 40 Bluebell — Harebell
### Campanula rotundifolia

Bluebell decorates the rocks on sand
dunes, seeming to grow right out of them.
But you will also find it on rocky slopes,
fields and open woods where it seems to
grow taller, up to a foot and a half high.
The bell-like flower nods from the top of
wire-slim stems with slender leaves that
suggest fragility.

## 41 Sheep Laurel — Lamb Kill
Kalmia angustifolia

When the Sheep Laurel blooms in late May and June, it turns our northern fields and swamps into pink gardens. The flowers grow below a top set of leaves, unlike the Swamp Laurel (27) where the flowers are on the end of the stem. It is said to be harmful, even fatal, to cows and sheep who are tempted to eat the fresh green leaves when there is nothing else around.

## 42 Daisy Fleabane
Erigeron philadelphicus

The heads of the Daisy Fleabane have yellow disks surrounded by purplish rays, and are worth examining closely. In case you try to count the number of thread-like rays in one head and have to give up, they are estimated at between a hundred and a hundred and fifty. The plant grows from six to twenty inches and blooms in fields and open woods.

## 43 Wild Calla
Calla palustris

The Wild Calla is an exotic and tropical-looking plant. It's exciting to come across it in bogs and small ponds. The milky-white spathe surrounds the golden spadix, and both are set off by the bright green heart-shaped leaves. After the flowers are finished, clusters of lovely red berries appear. The ground-up root has been used for making bread.

## 44 Field Mustard
Brassica

The Field Mustard is a bad weed and a nuisance to farmers. It is said that once the plant is established, the seeds can last as long as fifteen years and are very hard to clear out. Nevertheless, if in mid-summer you come upon a whole field of mustard waving in the breeze, it is a sight you'll remember. It is often cooked as a spring green and is even raised in some European countries for this purpose.

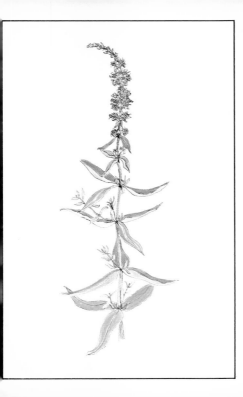

## 45 Purple Loosestrife
Lythrum salicaria

When the ditches are filled with Purple Loosestrife in bloom during July and August, it is a treat to drive along the highways. It is happily a common sight since the seeds are carried far and wide by the ditch waters. Originally brought from Europe, it grows up to four feet high.

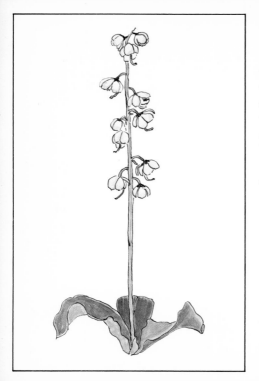

## 46 Shinleaf
Pyrola elliptica

In summer, the lovely little whitish-pink flowers of the Shinleaf appear in the woods. They have a waxy look and a sweet smell. The straight stalks grow from only five to ten inches from rounded green leaves that clasp the base. You will find it spread right across the northern United States, in wooded areas.

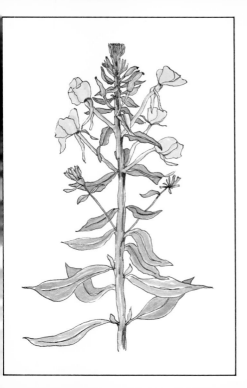

## 47 Evening Primrose
Oenothera biflora

It is not surprising that the evening primrose is a favorite flower of poets for it is a flower of the evening. As the heat of the day passes, its lovely clear yellow flowers open and give off a delicious perfume that seems to increase in intensity as the sun sinks. Although I have read that it can be grown from seed, I have never found a way to transplant it. If dug up, even when potted and watered, it wilts within minutes. That it seems only happy when growing wild makes it all the more romantic. Look for it in waste places, ditches and open fields.

## 48 Pipsissewa
Chimaphila umbellata

This little plant that never grows taller than twelve inches is a delight to come upon in the dark damp woods in July and August. Its small pink waxy flowers stand out against the shiny dark green leaves which are evergreen. Its Latin name *Chimaphila* means "winter loving." The Indians made a potion from the roots which they believed cured rheumatism.

## 49 Wild Rose
Rosa

This Wild Rose escaped from early gardens to establish itself along fences, beside railroad tracks and on beaches. The leaves are wrinkled, the stems prickly, and the large rose-colored or white flowers bloom from July to Setpember on a bushy shrub from two to six feet high. The rose hips can be used in making jelly and are a good source of Vitamin C. The Rose is the flower of New York State, and the Wild Rose is Iowa's state flower.

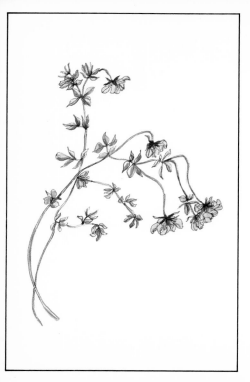

## 50 Birdfoot Trefoil
*Lotus corniculatus*

The yellow blooms of this trefoil are a very
cheerful sight from July to September. The
plant, however, is rather untidy, sprawling
from six to twenty-four inches. It will grow
in almost any soil, so you often find it in
waste places along roadsides that cannot
nurture other flowers. The pods suggest
a bird's foot, hence its name.

## 51 Heal All
Prunella vulgaris

This little flower — belonging to the mint family — is found all over North America. Early settlers believed it cured wounds and sore throats, hence its name. It flowers all summer long, and adapts itself to survive attacks. For instance, if it's cut down with a lawn-mower it simply grows back lower and thicker.

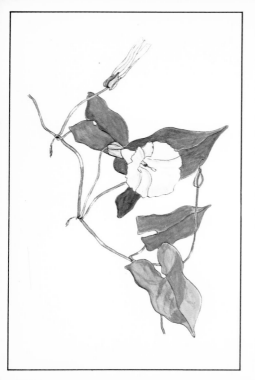

## 52 Hedge Bindweed
Convolvulus sepium

Hedge Bindweed is a wild morning glory that closes in the evening and opens around three o'clock in the morning. The flowers can be white or pink and the vine is particularly fond of roadside fences, where it blooms from June to September. The arrow shape of the large leaves distinguishes it from other members of the morning glory family. Pigs love to eat the roots and will dig them up if allowed, but the food has a purgative effect on them.

## 53 Nightshade, Bittersweet
Solanum dulcamara

Nightshade surprisingly belongs to the tomato family, but it is poisonous. It grows almost anywhere, but seems to prefer abandoned places. An unusual feature is that it has blue-purple flowers and berries that start off green and change to very bright red, growing on the vine at the same time from May to September.

## 54 Early Meadow-rue
Thalictrum dioicum

The little pom-poms of thread-thin stamens
that make up the flowers on this pretty
plant usually start off white in June, but
turn mauve as the season progresses. Its
leaves are particularly attractive and resemble
the maidenhair fern, and it blooms in sugar
maple woods at the same time as trilliums
and dog-toothed violets.

## 55 Hound's Tongue
Cynoglossum officinale

Pretty little maroon flowers decorate
this member of the forget-me-not family.
It is supposed to smell like a mouse nest,
but I have never smelled one so I don't
know if this is true. The fruit is covered
with sticky burrs that cling to clothes.
The leaves resemble a dog's tongue —
hence its name. Look for it in May and
June. It was once used as an anesthetic.

## 56 Fireweed
Epilobium angustifolium

This may be a weed, but when in bloom, and especially when growing with chicory, it makes a lovely sight. The pinky-purple flowers may be as high as seven feet in July and August. It grows in open places and in areas swept by fire, hence its English name. The young leaves and shoots may be eaten like asparagus, and the roots were cooked by the Indians to make a cure for boils.

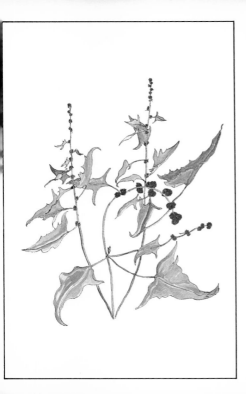

## 57 Strawberry Goosefoot
Chenopodium capitatum

In June, an insignificant white flower appears on this plant but after that come the bright red berries, easy to see against the green leaves. The plant grows in dry soil, in the woods and in cleared places. Children love to pick and eat the berries. In France, the berry is used to color wine that has turned out to be too pale.

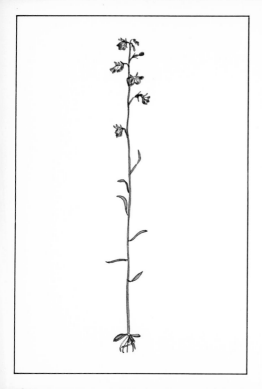

## 58 Brook Lobelia
Lobelia kalmii

The lobelia belongs to the bluebell family.
This dainty Brook Lobelia is so-called
because it grows in rich wet places, such
as on beaches, and along streams and
damp meadows. The tiny blue flowers
with a white center sparkle and attract
attention from mid-July to September.
The stem can be anywhere from four to
sixteen inches tall.

### 59 Black-eyed Susan
Rudbeckia hirta

Many consider the Black-eyed Susan the prettiest of all the wild flowers. It blooms in dry fields and along open roadsides from July to September. It is a member of the daisy family and reaches a height of up to three feet.

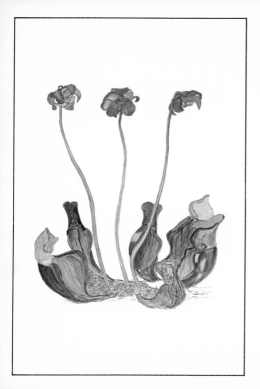

## 60 Pitcher Plant
Sarracenia purpurea

The Pitcher Plant is unique and immediately recognizable. A dull red flower nods from the top of a separate stalk, while the pitcher-like leaves are usually half-filled with water, and the lip lined with bristles that trap flies which are then digested by the enzymes. Look for it in sphagnum bogs from June to August. The brilliant green of the moss contrasts beautifully with the dull red blossom. The Indians made a potion from the plant to fight smallpox.

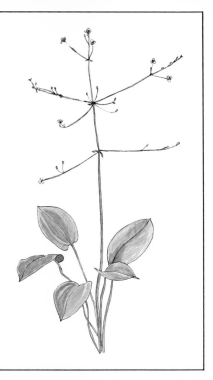

## 61 Water Plantain
*Alisma triviale*

The Water Plantain is a delicate plant growing in shallow muddy waters with a miniature flower that is a small-sized variation of the Arrowhead (**64**). Look for it from June to September in wet places. Like most plants that grow in water, it is widespread throughout the country.

## 62 Chicory, Blue Sailors
Cichorium intybus

The clear bright blue of the Chicory flower
appears in August to brighten the fields.
The heads open in the morning, turn toward
the sun as it moves, and are often closed by
noon. In Europe, it is cultivated and the
roots used to make a coffee substitute.
French restaurants are fond of adding a
pinch to their regular coffee. The Indians
used to boil the root for a beverage also.
Look for it in waste places, in open fields
and along roadsides. It grows as high as
four feet.

## 63 Grass of Parnassus
Parnassia

This belongs to the Saxifrage family of flowers that includes hydrangeas and miterworts (31). The lovely flower grows elegantly from the top of a leafless stem that may be as tall as two feet. The flower which blooms at the end of July is white, veined with pale green.

## 64 Broadleaved Arrowhead
Sagittaria latifolia

This is the commonest plant of the arrow-head family. The bright green arrow-shaped leaves can be seen pushing out of the mud in bogs, ponds and small streams. The white flowers bloom in July and August and are in clusters of three that wave above the leaves on straight stalks. Musk-rats and beavers love to eat the roots. These produce potato-like tubers that can be harvested in late fall. When roasted they taste like potatoes, but sweeter.

## 65 Closed Gentian
Gentiana andrewsii

This beautiful blue flower has petals that stay closed at the top of a rather stiff one to two-foot stem. It blooms in August and September and is rather hard to find. Look for it in wet fields, beside lakes and high on hills. Thoreau writes of finding them in quantity on September 28, 1858, but they seem to have declined considerably in number since then.

## 66 Turtlehead
Chelone glabra

The swollen two-lipped white flower which resembles a turtle with its mouth shut gives this plant its name. It grows in wet places, ditches and streams to a height of three feet and blooms from the end of July to September. Sometimes the flowers are pink.

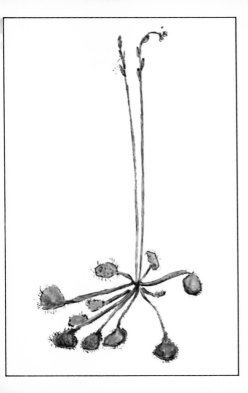

## 67 Roundleaved Sundew
Drosera rotundifolia

A very interesting little plant that eats insects. It grows only four to ten inches high in sphagnum bogs or wet acid soil and blooms from June to August. The round leaves are covered with red hairs and the end of each hair has a gland which exudes a sticky substance that looks like a dewdrop shining in the sunlight. When an insect goes near, it gets trapped and the substance acts as a gastric juice, helping the tissues of the leaves to digest as much of the insect as it can. The flowers may be pink or white.

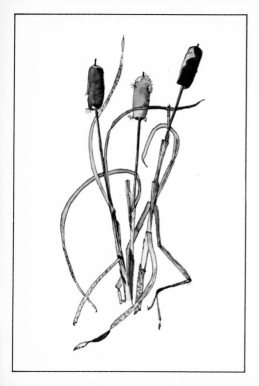

## 68 Broadleaved Cattail
Typha latifolia

Cattails, often mistakenly called bulrushes, grow to a height of nine feet in very wet ditches, swamps and marshes, and are among the most handsome and useful of our wild flowers. This plant is called the "supermarket of the swamps," because almost all of it is edible. The Indians made a sweet flour from the roots for bread and puddings, dried the tops and used them as torches, wove baskets from the long leaves, and used the pale down that later comes out of the flower to soften the inside of cradles. Blackbirds like to nest among the large clusters, and geese and muskrats eat the roots.

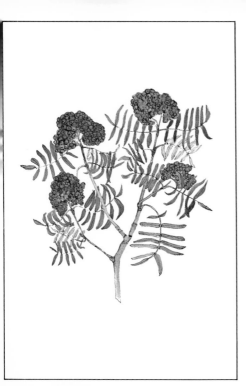

## 69 Mountain Ash
Pyrus decora

This is, of course, not a wild flower but a large shrub or small tree. In spring its branches bear white flowers, and the red berries that appear in autumn last the winter — making it a lovely sight against white snow.

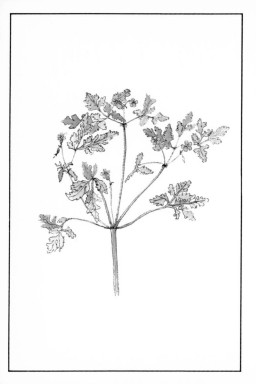

## 70 Herb Robert
Geranium robertanium

This small hairy plant grows in damp rocky woods across the northern U.S. It has a strong scent and belongs to the geranium family. It was named after St. Robert.

## 71 Northern Willow Herb
Epilobium glandulosum

This small delicate willow herb has tiny pink flowers that bloom from July to September. Look for it in wettish places.

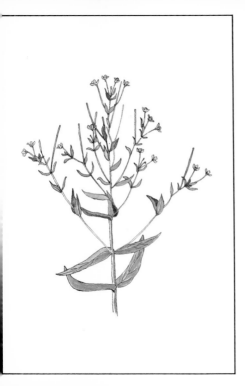

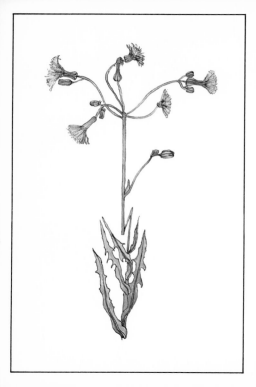

## 72 Smooth Hawksbeard
*Crepis capillaris*

Hawksbeard looks like a dandelion, but the heads of flowers grow in all directions from the end of the stem. It's an untidy plant, but its sunny yellow color does brighten our fields in summer. It also helps cheer up dry waste places where other plants won't grow. What do you think of its name?

## 73 Goldenrod
Solidago

Along with the daisy and the dandelion, the goldenrod is probably our most easily recognized wild flower. Classifying it however is another matter. There are more than 60 different species and since professional botanists often have trouble identifying each of them precisely, perhaps I may be forgiven for not being sure about this one. A field of goldenrod waving in the late August sun is a distinctly North American sight, and an incredibly beautiful one — even though some people believe it's to be sneezed at. The goldenrod is the state flower of Nebraska and Kentucky.

## 74 Milkweed
Asclepias syriaca

Milkweed is one of the most useful of our
wild flowers — from bud to flower to seed
pod. It got its name from the white, sticky
juice that runs from its stem. Nursing
mothers used to drink this juice, believing
that it increased the flow of milk for their
babies. When the little green buds appear,
they may be picked, boiled and eaten. When
the pinkish flowers bloom, they give off a
lovely perfume. Indians collected the dew
from the flowers to sweeten wild strawberries. The seed pods are filled with
silky fibers intended to carry the seeds
on the wind. The fibers were used by
early homesteaders to stuff cushions
and during both wars to fill lifejackets.

## 75 Virgin's Bower or Wild Clematis
Clematis virginiana

If you want to find wild bees, this is the flower to keep your eyes on. It is a vine that winds itself around trees and shrubs in the woods and along ditches. In August, the great profusions of white flowers are often smothered with bees. When the fruit forms, the vine is even more spectacular. The seeds are joined by silken threads and these curl around each other, making shiny, silken balls, lovely when the sun hits them and giving the plant another name — "Old Man's Beard."

## 76 Wild Columbine
Aquilegia canadensis

There was once a movement to make the
Columbine the national floral emblem of
the United States, because its popular name
suggested Columbia and its Latin name
*aquilia* meant eagle. But some believe the
Latin name comes from *aqua* for "water"
and *legere,* "to collect," because the flower
is shaped like a water holder. In any case
when the Columbine grows out of rocky
slopes in springtime, it is a very cheery sight.
Bees don't collect the nectar in the brightly
colored flowers, but hummingbirds do.

## 77 Red Baneberry
Actaea rubra

In May and June, the Red Baneberry blooms
in woods right across the northern United
States. The White Baneberry is also
common. The berries are very pretty —
bright red, or pure white with a black spot
(often called Doll's Eyes). They are poisonous, but since they taste so unpleasant, one
is not likely to eat them.

## 78 Black Knapweed
Centaurea nigra

This roadside plant that blooms from July
to September escaped from gardens in
Europe to cross the Atlantic and run wild
here. An old English poem describes how
a village maiden in England would pull
the little threads out of the button heads
and put the husk in a hanky in her bosom.
When the lad she loved passed by, they
burst out with new flowers.

### 79 Orange Hawkweed or Devil's Paint Brush
Hieracium aurantiacum

Farmers hate this weed and damn it with
the name Devil's Paint Brush. But its bright
orange head gives color to dried up areas
— it opens in the morning and closes toward
noon. The flowers also close when picked,
which is a pity since they would add an unusual touch to bouquets. Cattle won't eat
them, but it is believed that hawks do to
improve their eyesight. The Greek word for
hawk is *hierax.*

## 80 Moosewood, Hobblebush, Witch-hobble
Viburnum alnifolium

This lovely shrub is commonly called Moose-
wood because its branches remind one vague-
ly of moose's antlers. Look for it in the
woods and be pleased when you find it. It
is a native North American plant, and Euro-
peans have been trying to introduce it into
their gardens since 1820 but it seems to
grow happily only here. If you cut a little
branch that has a flower head on it in March
you can bring it indoors, put it in water and
it will bloom for you. But don't be greedy.
One spray is plenty.

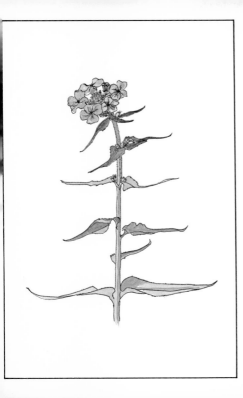

## 81 Dame's Rocket
Hesperis matronalis

This pretty purple flower looks like phlox, but it has only four petals to the phlox's five. It escaped from gardens to run wild along roadsides, in ditches and on the edges of woods, but it is so attractive gardeners continue to cultivate it. It flowers in early spring and gives off its fragrance towards evening.

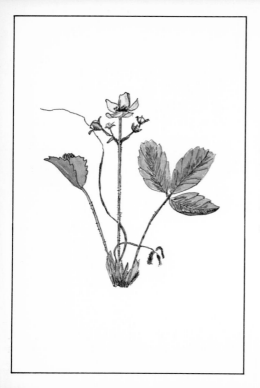

## 82 Wild Strawberry
Fragaria virginiana

The delight of coming across wild strawberries unexpectedly is a childhood experience remembered all one's life. Since their taste is as fresh and tangy as their color is lovely, it's hard to collect enough to bring home, and even harder to keep them long enough to cook. Those who succeed know they have the queen of jams. Look for the wild strawberry in dry fields and sandy places, along roadsides and railway tracks. The lovely white flower is as dainty as a violet.

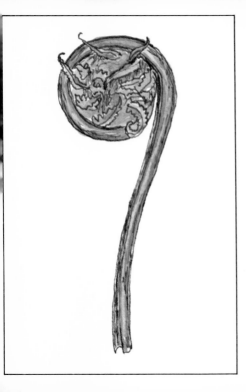

## 83 Fiddlehead of the Ostrich Fern
Matteuccia struthiopteris

This is really one of the largest and most graceful ferns, and not a flower at all. But in early May when the fiddlehead pushes through the earth, it looks as pretty as a flower. It is also very good to eat. If picked when it is between three and six inches high, washed in three fresh waters, then fried with bacon, it is a fine delicacy. Luckily, picking the fiddlehead does not ruin the fern, as more shoots come up from the root. Its name — in case you have not already guessed — comes from its resemblance to the end of a violin.

## THE WILD ORCHIDS

The rarest and most prized of all the wild flowers are the orchids. Not only does one never, never pick a wild orchid, but one does not tell where or when an orchid has been found in case somebody goes and picks it. Once in a while one comes across an unexpected mass of them, and then one feels privileged indeed.

### 84 White Bog Orchis
Habenaria dilatata

The White Bog Orchis grows in small stream and wet fields and has a lovely smell to go with its good looks. It has long slender leaves, and the lip of the flower is the same length as the spur. Look for this white or pale green flower in July.

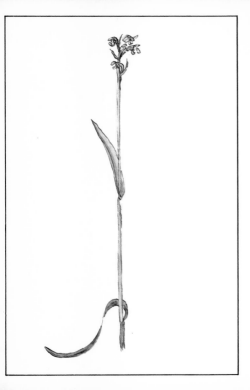

### 85 Small Woodland Orchis
Habenaria clavellata

The lip of this orchid is three-toothed at the apex. Flowers are greenish-white and bloom in July. Look for it in bogs and wet woods. It rarely grows more than a foot high.

## 86 Ladies' Tresses
Spiranthes romanzoffiana

A delicate little orchid, growing only
six to eighteen inches high, with flowers
spiralling around the stem. It blooms in
late July and August in fields and sandy
soil, and the white flowers do not nod.
Usually you will find it close by the
little grape fern.

## 87 Pink Lady's Slipper
Cypripedium acaule

The Pink Lady's Slipper is one of the most common members of the orchid family growing in the northern part of the country. In June you may come upon great masses of it when walking in the open pine woods, and a lovely sight it is. Even though they seem plentiful, the flowers should not be picked, nor even transplanted, as they will seldom survive a change of habitat more than a few years.

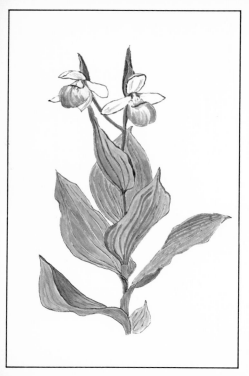

## 88 Showy Lady's Slipper
Cypripedium reginae

If you are lucky enough to find this beautiful orchid — the largest of all our northern orchids — you are likely to see hundreds of them growing together. They like very wet places, preferring mossy swamps and the same kind of rich earth as cedar trees. The plant is tall for an orchid, sometimes three feet high, with big veined leaves and purple and white flowers that bloom in July. Tiny hairs cover the plant and these contain a substance irritable to the skin and probably equally irritable to animals since they will not touch it.

## 89 Small Purple-fringed Orchis
Habenaria psycodes

A fragrant little orchid about a foot to three feet high, that grows in fields and swampy places, blooming in July. The purple flowers are fringed and delicate-looking. Always fairly rare, it caused Thoreau to ask why it grew so hidden away from where men usually walk.

## 90 White-fringed Orchis
Habenaria blephariglottis

Consider yourself very lucky if you come across this lovely orchid, as it is now very rare. The fringe around the lip makes it quite distinctive. It grows in sphagnum moss, near bogs, and in very wet fields, and blooms in July.

# Index — English

# Index — Latin